MONTICELLO PUBLIC LIBRARY
512 E. LAKE AVE.
MONTICELLO, WI 53570

# HOW & WHY ?

# PLANTS EAT INSECTS

MONTICELLO PUBLIC LIBRARY
512 E. LAKE AVE.

Elaine Pascoe is the author of more than 20 acclaimed children's books on a wide range of subjects.
Dwight Kuhn's scientific expertise and artful eye work together with the camera to capture the awesome wonder of the natural world.

**Please visit our web site at: www.garethstevens.com**
**For a free color catalog describing Gareth Stevens Publishing's list of high-quality books**
**and multimedia programs, call 1-800-542-2595 or fax your request to (414) 332-3567.**

**Library of Congress Cataloging-in-Publication Data**

Pascoe, Elaine.
    Plants eat insects / by Elaine Pascoe; photographs by Dwight Kuhn. — North American ed.
      p. cm. — (How & why: a springboards into science series)
    Includes bibliographical references and index.
    Summary: Explains how and why pitcher plants, sundews, and other carnivorous plants
trap insects for food.
    ISBN 0-8368-3011-3 (lib. bdg.)
    1. Carnivorous plants—Juvenile literature. [1. Carnivorous plants.] I. Kuhn, Dwight, ill. II. Title.
QK917.P37   2002
583.75—dc21                                     2001049485

This North American edition first published in 2002 by
**Gareth Stevens Publishing**
A World Almanac Education Group Company
330 West Olive Street, Suite 100
Milwaukee, WI 53212 USA

First published in the United States in 2000 by Creative Teaching Press, Inc., P.O. Box 2723, Huntington Beach, CA 92647-0723.
Text © 2000 by Elaine Pascoe; photographs © 2000 by Dwight Kuhn. Additional end matter © 2002 by Gareth Stevens, Inc.

Gareth Stevens editor: Mary Dykstra
Gareth Stevens designer: Tammy Gruenewald

All rights to this edition reserved to Gareth Stevens, Inc. No part of this book may be reproduced, stored in a retrieval system, or transmitted in any form or by any means, electronic, mechanical, photocopying, recording, or otherwise, without the prior written permission of the publisher, except for the inclusion of brief quotations in an acknowledged review.

Printed in the United States of America

1 2 3 4 5 6 7 8 9 06 05 04 03 02

# HOW & WHY ?

# PLANTS EAT INSECTS

by Elaine Pascoe
photographs by Dwight Kuhn

A SPRINGBOARDS INTO
SCIENCE
SERIES

**Gareth Stevens Publishing**
A WORLD ALMANAC EDUCATION GROUP COMPANY

MONTICELLO PUBLIC LIBRARY
512 E. LAKE AVE.
MONTICELLO, WI 53570

Pitcher plants poke up through the damp ground. They are called "pitcher plants" because each plant is shaped like a little pitcher, and it holds water. Pitcher plants are even more unusual than they look. These plants eat insects!

Sometimes a frog visits a pitcher plant. Both the frog and the plant are waiting for the same thing — a tasty insect meal.

Insects and spiders visit pitcher plants searching for food. But when they go into the plants, they cannot climb out. The inside of the pitcher is slippery, and it is lined with tiny spines. All of the spines point downward.

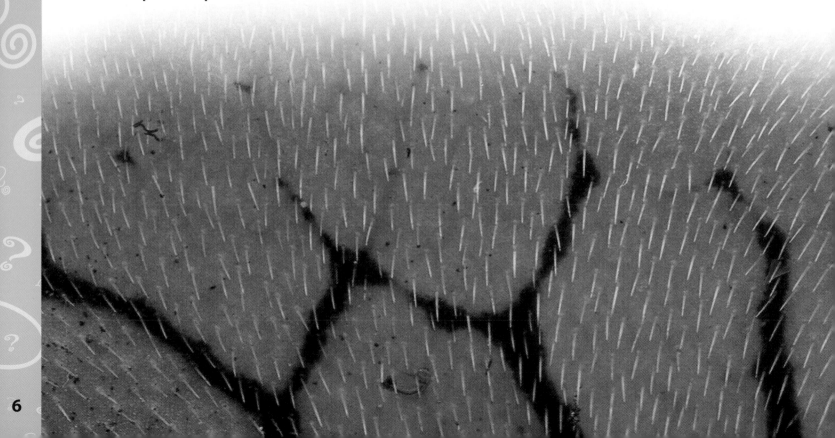

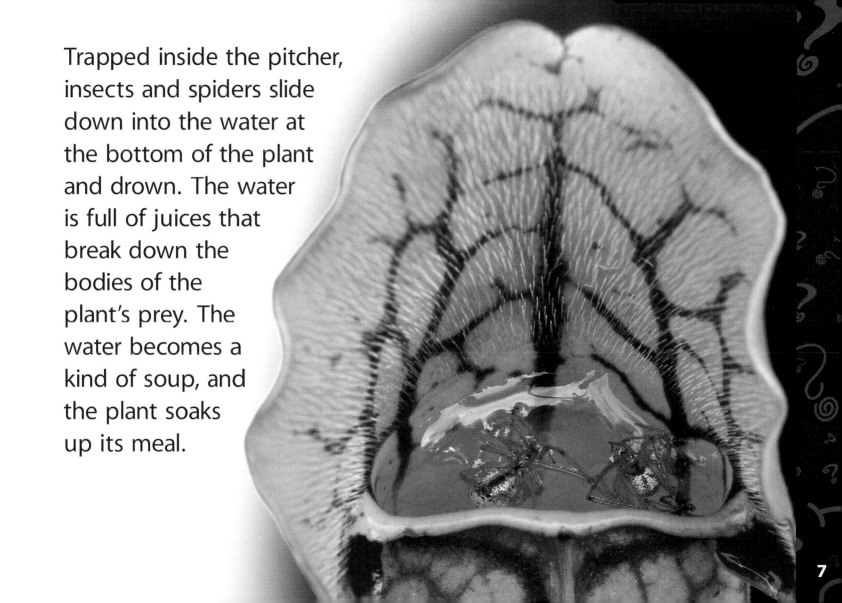

Trapped inside the pitcher, insects and spiders slide down into the water at the bottom of the plant and drown. The water is full of juices that break down the bodies of the plant's prey. The water becomes a kind of soup, and the plant soaks up its meal.

Sundews grow in boggy places, where the soil is poor. Like other insect-eating plants, sundews need more nourishment than they can get from the soil. So they get what they need from insects.

The sundew sets a sweet trap. The plant's leaves are covered with reddish hairs. The hairs are coated with sticky juice.

The sundew's juice smells sweet, so insects, such as this flower fly, come to drink. Once an insect lands, it cannot leave. The juice is too sticky. The sundew is like a living piece of flypaper! As the insect struggles, the sundew's sticky hairs bend to hold it tight. Then the hairs begin to make digestive juices. In a few days, only the shell of the insect is left.

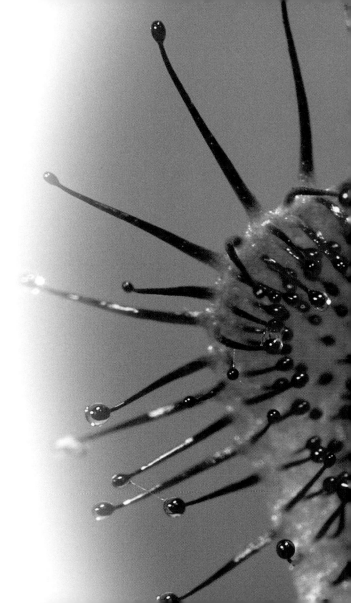

A Venus flytrap captures insects with a snap! This plant's leaves look almost like flowers. They are shiny and red inside, and they have lots of sweet nectar.

Each leaf has a fringe of delicate spines. These spines are very important to the plant. They tell it when a meal arrives.

A damselfly, for example, might come to a Venus flytrap, searching for nectar. When the damselfly lands on a leaf, it brushes against special trigger hairs.

Snap! The leaf closes tightly, trapping the damselfly inside.
Juices flow from the leaf, breaking down the damselfly's body.
The leaf will not open until it has soaked up its insect meal.

Bladderworts grow underwater in ponds. These plants are covered with tiny air-filled sacs. The sacs look like bubbles, but they are actually traps. Water fleas, mosquito larvae, and other tiny water insects come to the plants, looking for food.

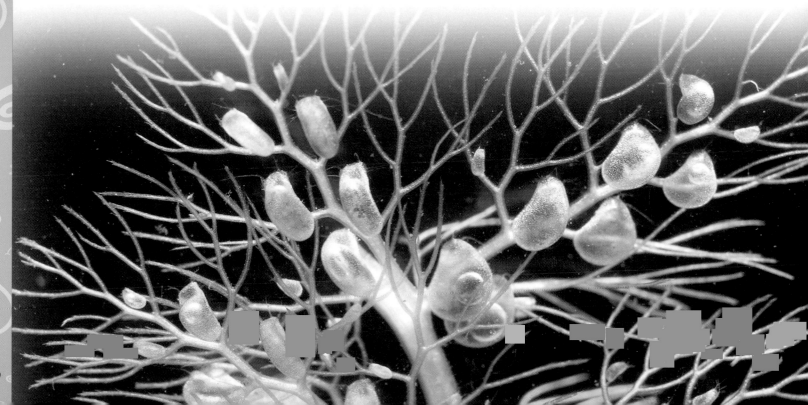

When an insect brushes against a bubble trap, the trap springs open. Water rushes into the bubble, bringing the insect with it. Then the trap shuts. Plant juices flow into the bubble to break down the insect, and the bladderwort has a meal.

# Can you answer these "HOW & WHY" questions?

**1.** How did the pitcher plant get its name?

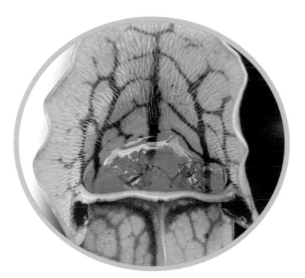

**2.** Why do insects and spiders crawl into a pitcher plant?

**3.** Why do sundews and other insect-eating plants need nourishment from insects?

**4.** Why can't an insect leave a sundew leaf after landing on it?

**5.** How does a Venus flytrap catch an insect?

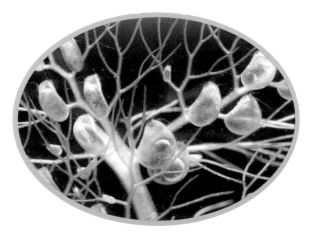

**6.** How does a bladderwort use water to catch insects?

MONTICELLO PUBLIC LIBRARY
512 E. LAKE AVE.
MONTICELLO, WI 53570

*(See page 20 for answers.)*

# ANSWERS

1. A pitcher plant is shaped like a pitcher you might find in your kitchen, and it holds water, too.

2. Insects and spiders, attracted by a pitcher plant's sweet smell, crawl into the plant to look for food.

3. Insect-eating plants typically live in swampy places, in soil that does not provide enough nourishment, so these plants need to eat insects for nourishment.

4. The reddish hairs on a sundew leaf are covered with juice that is so sticky it traps any unlucky insect that lands on the leaf.

5. When an insect brushes against the trigger hairs on the leaf of a Venus flytrap, the leaf snaps shut, trapping the insect.

6. When an insect brushes against one of the bladderwort's tiny, air-filled sacs, or "bubble traps," water rushes into the sac, bringing the insect in with it.

## Feed Me!

Visit a greenhouse or a plant store to see if it sells any types of insect-eating plants. You can also look for these unusual plants at a conservatory, which is a place that displays plants for visitors to see. What would a person taking care of these plants have to do to keep them healthy? How would you feed an insect-eating plant that is grown indoors? If possible, ask plant experts at the greenhouse or conservatory to show you how they care for insect-eating plants.

## Where in the World

Venus flytraps are found only in the United States, but pitcher plants and bladderworts can be found in many parts of the world. Use books or the Internet to learn about the varieties of insect-eating plants found around the world. For example, an African species of sundew has leaves that are 2 feet (0.6 meter) long! Make a chart showing all of the continents and listing the species of insect-eating plants that can be found on each continent.

## Invent an Insect-eater

Use your imagination to invent a new kind of insect-eating plant. Think about what your plant would look like and how it would capture insects. Draw a picture of your plant, using crayons or markers to show what colors it would be. Then, make up a name for your plant and print the name under the plant's picture. Add a few sentences explaining how this new species of insect-eating plant catches its food.

# GLOSSARY

**boggy:** having wet, spongy, mucky soil.

**coated:** covered with a thick liquid.

**delicate:** easily damaged or broken.

**digestive:** related to digestion, which is the process of breaking down food for use by the body.

**flypaper:** a type of paper that has a sticky coating on it for catching and killing flies.

**fringe:** a border or edging with dangling threads or thin strips that hang downward.

**larvae:** the wingless, wormlike forms of some insects when they first hatch from their eggs.

**nectar:** the sweet liquid in flowers that many insects and birds like to drink.

**nourishment:** substances that plants and animals need to grow and stay healthy.

**poke (v):** to push or jab with a pointed object, such as a stick or a finger.

**ponds:** bodies of water that are smaller than lakes.

**sacs:** parts of a plant or an animal that are shaped like small bags or pouches.

**searching:** looking for something or someone in a very careful way.

**shell:** a hard outer covering.

**soaks up:** takes in or absorbs.

**spines:** stiff, sharp, hairlike growths that stick out like thorns.

**trapped:** caught in a place or a device with no way to escape.

**trigger hairs:** the sensitive hairs on the leaf of a Venus flytrap that cause the leaf to close when they are touched by an insect.

## More Books to Read

*Bloodthirsty Plants* (series). Victor Gentle (Gareth Stevens)

*Flytrap. Living Things* (series). Rebecca Stefoff (Marshall Cavendish)

*Hungry Plants*. Mary Batten (Golden Books)

*Plants Bite Back!* Richard Platt (DK Publishing)

*Plants That Eat Animals*. Allan Fowler (Children's Press)

*Venus Flytraps*. Kathleen V. Kudlinski (Lerner)

## Videos

*Eyewitness: Plant*. (DK Vision)

*The Venus's-Flytrap*. (Encyclopedia Britannica Educational Corp.)

*The World of Insectivorous Plants*. (Films for the Humanities & Sciences)

## Web Sites

www.botany.org/bsa/misc/carn.html

www.geocities.com/RainForest/Vines/8358/vnta.html

www.ucalgary.ca/~dmjacobs/edts325/flytrap/homepage.htm

Some web sites stay current longer than others. For additional web sites, use a good search engine to locate the following topics: *carnivorous plants* and *insect-eating plants*.

# INDEX